The Bayeux Tapestry

TEXT:
Pierre Bouet and François Neveux

CONTENTS

Editions OUEST-FRANCE

Introduction

The Bayeux Tapestry is actually an embroidery in wool yarn on a linen cloth that measures roughly 70 m in length. It used to be thought that the work was created by Queen Matilda, wife of William the Conqueror (1028-1087), but in all probability it was commissioned by William's half-brother Odo, Bishop of Bayeux. After the victory at Hastings, Odo became the second in power in the kingdom, acting as viceroy in the absence of his brother. He was given several estates in England, as well as the county of Kent. This county, like the rest of the country, had many embroidery workshops. Moreover,

the monks at the cathedral and at St Augustine's Abbey in Canterbury produced illuminated manuscripts in their scriptoriums, and some of their illustrations were used as templates by designers and embroiderers. The majority of specialists now believe that the Tapestry was made in England, probably in Canterbury, by a team of English and Norman embroiderers. The Latin text of the *tituli*, or captions, is influenced by both Anglo-Saxon and Old French.

This embroidery is a pictorial depiction of the conquest of England. It starts with Harold's mission to Normandy and William's military

↓Odo, who probably commissioned the Bayeux Tapestry (scenes 43-44).

2

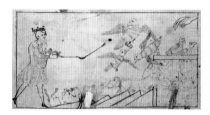

↑and →The scene showing a man hunting with a sling (scene 10) is based on an illustration from the Canterbury manuscript.
British Library, *Cotton Claudius* B, IV, folio 26v.

↓Harold and his companion in prayer in Bosham church (scene 3).

expedition to Brittany, in around 1064. We then see Harold swearing an oath to the Duke of Normandy. The Tapestry goes on to portray the death of Edward and Harold's coronation as King of England on 6 January 1066. The second part shows the preparations for the invasion, the Norman army crossing the Channel and the Battle of Hastings, which culminates in the death of Harold.

Strangely, the Tapestry portrays Harold in a favourable light, which can only be explained by the fact that it was produced shortly after the conquest, sometime between 1067 and 1070. During this early period, William applied a policy of reconciliation between victors and defeated, but this approach was discarded after the large-scale Anglo-Saxon revolts in 1069 and 1070.

We can only really grasp the full meaning of this remarkable work if we examine how it was made, the historical context and the events it reports, as compared with written sources. The Tapestry uses extremely subtle iconographic techniques to illustrate these events. But it nevertheless contains many unresolved mysteries, particularly in the upper and lower borders which frame the central scene. The Tapestry provides an unparalleled account of Western European civilisation in the second half of the 11th century. It is a miracle that it has been so well preserved, having survived the ravages of centuries, particularly the Wars of Religion, the French Revolution and the Second World War.

3

THE TEXTile work

The Bayeux Tapestry was so called in the early 18th century, in the first two publications on the work written by Antoine Lancelot and Dom Bernard de Montfaucon (who had not actually seen it!).

But strictly speaking it is not a tapestry; it is an embroidery in coloured wool yarn on an unbleached fine linen background. It is 68.38 m long and 48 to 51 cm high and is composed of nine panels joined together with fine stitching. The middle section, which depicts the historical account, is framed by two decorative borders, each 7 to 8 cm tall. The cloth is topped by a linen strip (later numbered from 1 to 58), which allowed it to be hung up on display in Bayeux Cathedral. The reverse side was protected by a lining.

The wool yarn used for the embroidery was coloured with three plant-based dyes: madder (red), weld (yellow) and woad (indigo blue). These were used either pure or in blends mixed by dyers, to produce around ten different colours with varied shades: red, yellow, beige, dark blue and green.

The embroiderers used four stitches. The main one was laid work, also known as "Bayeux stitch". This involves several steps: threads are laid across the surface of the fabric and are then covered with a second layer of threads at right angles, spaced at roughly 3 mm intervals; finally, small stitches are used to attach the threads to the fabric. This produces a slightly raised effect. The figures are outlined using stem stitch, which in some cases

↓ The four stitches are all used in this scene (scene 29): *stem stitch* to outline the characters and buildings and for the faces and captions; *laid work* to fill in the clothes and bodies; *chain stitch* for some of the letters in the caption – DED (ER) VNT HAROLD (O); and *split stitch* for the letter E in (DED) E (RVNT).

→ The thread used for the caption is covered by the threads used to embroider the helmet, indicating that the caption was stitched first (scene 19, reverse side).

↗ The trailing yarn shows that the embroiderers went from one image to the next.

↓ The end of the Tapestry, which has undergone extensive restoration (scene 58).

was actually completed first, before the images were "filled in". Stem stitch is also used for faces and hands and for the text that runs under the upper border. Chain stitch and split stitch are used to make some letters and linear motifs stand out more.

The Bayeux Tapestry has suffered from wear and tear and neglect over the years. The beginning and end of the embroidered cloth have been most affected. It has been repaired and restored several times, particularly since 1860. A total of 518 patches have been added, and the cloth has been strengthened in around a hundred places.

The Bayeux Tapestry is a unique piece, but it wasn't the only one of its kind in the Middle Ages. We know that many other works were produced to illustrate either the Battle of Hastings or other military episodes, such as the story of Byrhtnoth, who died in the Battle of Maldon against the Danish in 991. But the Bayeux embroidery is the only one to have reached us virtually intact. In his *Poème à Adèle* (Adela of Normandy, William the Conqueror's daughter), Baldric of Dol tells us that Princess Adela had a hanging similar to the Bayeux Tapestry displayed in her bedroom.

The HISTORICAL Context

The only way we can really grasp the importance of the Bayeux Tapestry and understand why it was produced is by looking at the historical context and the reasons for the Norman conquest of England after the death of Edward the Confessor in 1066. How did it come about that William the Bastard, Duke of Normandy, was able to lay claim to the throne of England?

ENGLAND AND THE NORDIC WORLD

Like the rest of Europe, England was attacked by Viking invaders on several occasions in the 9th and 10th centuries. In the early 11th century, the Danish waged a powerful attack, becoming masters of the entire kingdom in 1015. King Ethelred II (987-1016) died following this invasion and the throne, which had first been claimed by Sweyn, King of Denmark, passed to his son Canute. Ethelred's widow, Emma, was a Norman princess, the daughter of Richard I. She sent her children Alfred, Edward and Godgifu to safety in Rouen, Normandy. When she returned to England, she married King Canute, and they had a son, Harthacnut. Under the reign of Canute the Great

(1016-1035), England enjoyed a time of peace and prosperity. Canute governed England, Denmark and, from 1028, southern Norway. When he died, the crown of England passed to his sons, firstly Harold (1035-1040), son of Aelfgifu, then Harthacnut (1040-1042), son of Emma. Since Harthacnut had no heirs, he brought his half-brother Edward back to succeed him in 1042.

Edward had spent nearly thirty years in exile in Normandy, and he brought many Normans back with him to England to fill important positions. The new King married Edith, the daughter of Godwin, who was the most powerful man in the kingdom. But before his marriage, in 1053, he had already chosen his distant cousin, the young William of Normandy, to succeed him as King of England. Through his mother Emma, Edward was the first cousin of William's father, Robert the Magnificent, Duke of Normandy. This official appointment had even been approved by the Witenagemot, the advisory assembly of English aristocrats, and Wulfnoth, one of Godwin's sons, was sent to Rouen together with one of Godwin's grandsons, Hakon, as a guarantee of good faith. When Godwin died, he was succeeded by his son Harold.

→ Genealogy of the Dukes of Normandy and the Kings of England from 950 to 1135.

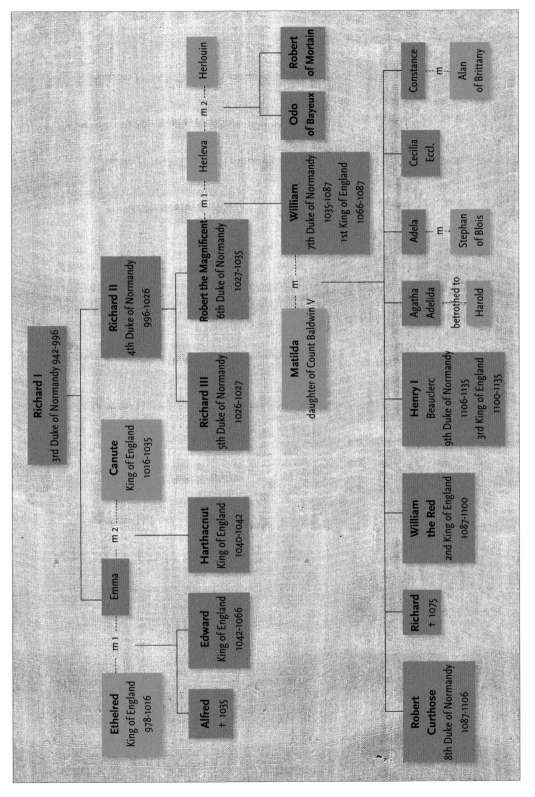

7

NORMANDY AND THE KINGDOM OF FRANCE

Across the Channel, Normandy was a territorial principality ruled by the young Duke William, known as William the Bastard. Although his father, Robert the Magnificent, had been Duke of Normandy, his mother, Herleva or Arlette, was the daughter of a tradesman from Falaise. When Robert died in 1035, William faced several challenges to his rule, because of his illegitimate birth and also because of his age (he was only eight years old). He had to call on King Henry I of France to help him establish his reign over the duchy. With Henry's backing, he defeated the rebels in the Battle of Val-ès-Dunes in 1047. In around 1050, William married Matilda, the daughter of Count Baldwin V of Flanders, forging an alliance with a rich territorial principality that was open to England and the Nordic countries. William was involved in long-standing conflicts with the Count of Anjou, Geoffrey Martel, and the King of France – who by now was beginning to feel threatened by the growing power of the Duchy of Normandy – and had to overcome two invasions, one in 1054 in Mortemer and the other in 1057 in Varaville. But

← Normandy and the Kingdom of France in the 11th century.

the death of both adversaries in 1060 removed these threats and left William free to turn Normandy into a virtually independent principality.

CLAIMANTS TO THE THRONE OF ENGLAND

In England, the reigning King was free to choose his successor, as long as he was from the same family line; he also had to ask for an opinion from the Witenagemot, the assembly of "wise men" in the kingdom. In around 1050, Edward chose William as his successor. Over several centuries, England and Normandy had developed economic, political and religious links; if Dudo of Saint-Quentin is to be believed, Rollo of Normandy offered assistance to a

↓ Genealogy of the Godwin family.

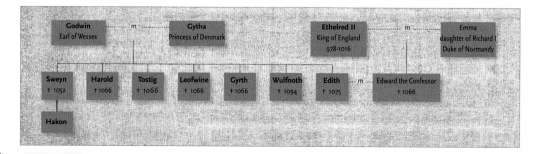

King of England on several occasions and in return the King offered to let him rule over half of his kingdom! The royal or princely dynasties on the continent were also linked by several marriage alliances to those in England. Emma of Normandy became Queen of England by marrying Ethelred and then Canute. William the Bastard therefore fulfilled the three criteria required for a legitimate claim to the throne: he had been chosen by the reigning King, he belonged to the same line and he had the approval of the "wise men".

The Duke of Normandy wasn't the only pretender to the English throne. There were four possible candidates. The first was an Anglo-Saxon prince, Edward, son of Edmund Ironside, who had reigned as King for less than a year in 1016. Edward was living in exile in Hungary with his family but was recalled to England by Edward the Confessor in 1057. It seems that the King may have changed his mind and preferred an English prince as his successor rather than William. But he died just a few weeks after arriving in London. His son Edgar was too young to become King at that stage, though he was considered for the role after the Battle of Hastings.

Early on in his reign, King Edward had thought of choosing the King of Denmark, Sweyn II Estridsen (1047-1076), as heir. This seemed a logical idea because previously, during the reigns of Canute and Harthacnut, the English and Danish kingdoms had been ruled by the same King. But in 1066, Sweyn II Estridsen, under threat from King Harald Hardrada of Norway, was not in a position to succeed Edward. He did try his luck after the victory at Hastings, however, sending his fleet to attack England on several occasions.

A more serious competitor was King Harald Hardrada of Norway (1047-1066), who had made his name as a mercenary in Constantinople. He even became commander of the personal guard of the Byzantine emperor. When he returned to Norway, he made a successful claim to the crown and then sought to extend his rule to Denmark. When Edward died, Harald laid claim to the throne of England on the basis of an old treaty between his predecessor, Magnus the Good, and King Harthacnut. In the summer of 1066, he prepared his fleet to invade the north of England.

The last of the serious contenders was Harold, the son of Godwin and brother-in-law of the King. Harold was a loyal supporter of King Edward, and since 1053 he had governed the kingdom of England under Edward's authority. He had proven himself as a strong military leader, winning several battles, particularly against Wales. He controlled the country by ruling directly over the vast earldom of Wessex and indirectly over the other earldoms through his brothers (Leofwine and Gyrth), his brothers-in-law (Edwin and Morcar) and his ally Waltheof. Although he swore fealty to William while he was in Normandy, he presumably hoped to become King of England himself, with or without Edward's agreement.

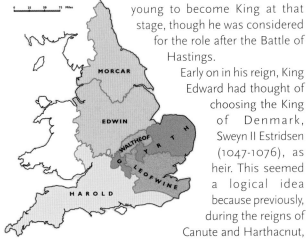

↓ Anglo-Saxon England in 1065.

The events as THEY Happened, according to the Tapestry and written sources

The Bayeux Tapestry is an important historical source that offers new insights over and above what we can learn from Latin and French written sources. In around 1070, the monk William of Jumièges wrote his Book VII about the early years of William the Conqueror and the conquest of England. In around 1075, William of Poitiers, a former knight of Duke William, wrote a lengthy biography about the Conqueror. And in around 1120, Orderic Vitalis, a monk at Saint-Evroul, provided a substantial account of William's English expedition in his *Historia Ecclesiastica*. Alongside these historical accounts, the poet Guy of Amiens, Queen Matilda's chaplain, wrote his *Carmen de Hastingae Proelio* (*Song of the Battle of Hastings*) in 1068. A century later, Wace, Canon of Bayeux, and Benoît de Sainte-Maure, both poets and chroniclers in the court of Henry II and Eleanor, each wrote a history of the Dukes of Normandy in Old French. On the English side, there is only one source in Old English, the *Anglo-Saxon Chronicle*, which was later followed by works in Latin written by the Anglo-Norman historians William of Malmesbury, John of Worcester and Henry of Huntingdon.

HAROLD'S MISSION

Harold, Earl of Wessex, was effectively governor of England on behalf of King Edward the Confessor. The King sent Harold on a mission to Normandy to confirm to Duke William that he

←Harold is taken prisoner by Guy of Ponthieu as soon as he lands (scene 7).

ET HIC: TRANSIERVNT :FLVMEN: COSNONIS: ET
HIC: HAROLD:DVX: TRAHEBAT: EO
DE ARENA

The Normans cross Mont Saint-Michel Bay on their way to Brittany (scenes 16-17).

had been chosen as heir to the throne of England. On his way to France he sailed into a storm and arrived on the shores of Ponthieu, where he was captured by Count Guy of Ponthieu, who hoped to negotiate a ransom. When William heard what had happened, he ordered Count Guy to hand over his prisoner, for a ransom, according to William of Poitiers. Anglo-Norman historians also mention the possibility of a fishing trip or a trip to Flanders.

↓ Harold saves an Englishman and a Norman from quicksand (scene 17).

THE EXPEDITION TO BRITTANY

Harold was received with pomp in Rouen by the Duke of Normandy. Orderic Vitalis writes that the Duke promised Harold one of his daughters in marriage; this may have been the mysterious Aelfgyva from scene 15 of the Tapestry. William took Harold with him to Brittany to assist him in his military campaign in support of a vassal who had rebelled against Conan II, Duke of Brittany. At the border, the Tapestry shows the first image of Mont Saint-Michel Abbey, which was nearing completion. As they crossed the shore, Harold rescued an Englishman and a Norman who were caught in quicksand. The Tapestry also provides information about the sieges of Rennes and Dinan, which the other sources don't mention. Concerning the siege of Dol, Conan is depicted fleeing the fortified city. William of Poitiers confirms that Conan had laid siege to the rebel town.

11

HAROLD'S OATH

On their return, the Duke showed his gratitude to Harold by rewarding him with arms, a scene that William of Poitiers actually situates before the Brittany campaign. In Bayeux, Harold "made an oath to Duke William" on sacred relics of the cathedral. William of Poitiers gives us more detail about this oath. He tells us that the Duke appointed Harold as his representative in England, making him promise to help William become King when Edward died. He adds that William made Harold his vassal and agreed to free Harold's nephew Hakon, who had been held hostage in Rouen since 1051. According to William of Poitiers, the oath was made in Bonneville-sur-Touques, whereas Orderic Vitalis writes that it occurred in Rouen. William of Jumièges explains that Harold swore "many oaths of fealty concerning the kingdom".

↓ Harold swears an oath to Duke William on sacred relics of Bayeux Cathedral (scene 23).

↑ Harold is crowned King of England by Archbishop Stigant (scene 30).

THE DEATH OF EDWARD AND THE CORONATION OF HAROLD

Shortly after Harold arrived back in England, King Edward fell ill. He died on 5 January 1066 and was buried in the new Westminster Abbey. On his deathbed, he named Harold as his successor. William of Poitiers confirms this bequest *in articulo mortis*, which was in accordance with the Roman law applied in England. The "wise men" of the kingdom approved the choice and offered the throne to Harold. Harold was crowned King by Stigant, Archbishop of Canterbury, on 6 January. Shortly after the coronation, the Tapestry shows a star (which was in fact Halley's Comet), which for a contemporary audience would have been a bad omen, signalling misfortune and upheavals.

13

OMISSIONS IN THE TAPESTRY

When William heard the news, he decided to organise a military campaign to assert his right to the throne of England. This required considerable preparation: food had to be transported to the base at Dives-sur-Mer, sufficient weapons and military equipment had to be produced, and the troops and horses had to be kept well supplied. The Tapestry doesn't show anything of these preparations other than the building of the ships required to transport the army and the invasion itself on 28 September.

The Tapestry remains silent about all the other important events that occurred during the summer of 1066 – it doesn't show the Norman fleet travelling from Dives to Saint-Valéry-sur-Somme on 12 September, nor does it depict the shipwreck of some of the boats at the bottom of the cliffs in the Pays de Caux, which William de Poitiers reports in detail.

Other written sources tell us that another claimant to the throne, Harald Hardrada, King of Norway, was also preparing to invade England. Around 15 September, Harald arrived on the north-eastern shores of England with a fleet of 360 ships. On 20 September, in Fulford, his army crushed the troops of Earls Edwin and Morcar, forcing Harold to make a hasty trip northwards from the southern coast to face the King of Norway. On 25 September, at Stamford Bridge, Harold won a decisive victory: Harald Hardrada

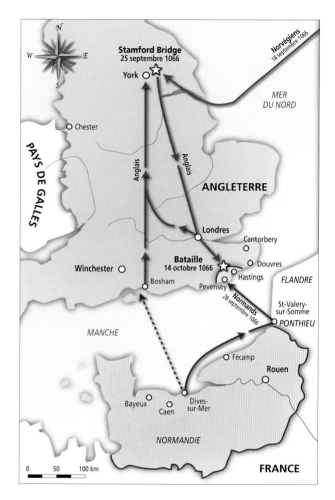

was defeated and killed. The Tapestry shows nothing of these events.

It seems likely that William waited for Harald to invade and for Harold to travel north. As soon as he received news of these events, he set sail by night, as William of Poitiers tells us, and landed unopposed in Pevensey on 29 September.

↑ Map showing military movements in September and October 1066.

THE NORMANS ARRIVE AND SETTLE IN ENGLAND

The Tapestry is a precious source of information about the Normans' actions after they landed in England, which the written texts don't mention. It shows the horses leaving the ships, followed by scenes of pillaging and houses being burnt down with women and children inside. We see bread and food being cooked and a meal for knights and dignitaries. At the same time, we see the motte-and-bailey castle being built in Hastings. But the Tapestry doesn't show anything of the negotiations that took place before the battle, which William of Poitiers recounts at length.

After these negotiations broke down, an armed conflict became inevitable. The two armies sent out scouts to detect enemy movements. Orderic Vitalis is the only source to indicate the precise location of the battlefield, on Senlac Hill (now known as Battle), 6 miles from Hastings.

↓ As soon as they arrive on English soil, the Normans set about pillaging (scenes 40-41).

15

THE BATTLE

The Tapestry starts by showing William urging his troops to fight "manfully and wisely", as the Latin caption tells us. William of Poitiers echoes this plea in more detail in his writings.

The embroidered work had no way of showing in pictures what the texts say about the composition of the two armies. On the Norman side, we know that William deployed his troops in three divisions: the Bretons on the left, the French and Flemish on the right, and the Normans in the centre. He also placed his archers on the front line, his foot soldiers behind them and his mounted knights at the back. On the English side, Harold deployed his elite troops, composed of *thegns* (noblemen) and *housecarls* (personal bodyguards of Scandinavian origin), in the centre. On the wings, he placed the troops from the *fyrd* (a levy of local peasants).

The Tapestry's designers chose to give priority to the cavalry rather than the infantry. The battle opposed mounted Norman soldiers, armed with lances, and English foot soldiers tightly packed together to form a "shield wall". The Tapestry picks out a few moments of bravery with which the contemporary public were familiar and which are also recorded in the written texts, but does not necessarily present them in chronological order. It shows the death of Harold's two brothers Leofwine and Gyrth, the dramatic fall of three horses, and unexpected resistance from some *fyrd* troops who took refuge on a hill.

Bishop Odo is then shown on horseback, armed with a club, which the caption tells us he is using to rally the young troops. But William of Poitiers tells us that Odo, Geoffrey de Montbray, Bishop of Coutances (not depicted on the Tapestry) and

↑ Norman knights face off against English foot soldiers (scene 51).

other clerics did not actually fight on the battlefield but instead prayed for victory.

The Tapestry shows William lifting his helmet to receive recognition from his men, following the rumour that he had been killed, which had led many troops to desert the battlefield.

→ The arrangement of the two armies before the start of the battle (14 October 1066, around 9am).

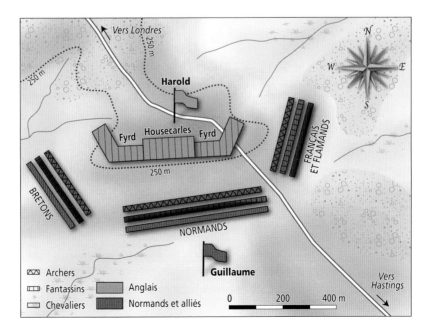

Vers Londres

250 m

250 m

Harold

Fyrd   Housecarles   Fyrd

FRANCAIS ET FLAMANDS

250 m

BRETONS

NORMANDS

Guillaume

Vers Hastings

Archers
Fantassins
Chevaliers

Anglais
Normands et alliés

0   200   400 m

17

HAROLD'S DEATH

The final scenes portray the final epi-sode in the battle. On the lower border, the Norman archers are seen advancing to try to bring their adversaries down with close-range direct fire, rather than the high-angle fire used at the beginning. This method proved effective, and Harold was struck in the eye by an arrow. This detail shown on the Tapestry is also recorded by an Italian chronicler, Amatus of Montecassino, in his *History of the Normans* (c. 1080), and by Baldric of Dol in his *Poème à Adèle* (c. 1100).

These tactics led to widespread confusion in the English ranks and frenzied hand-to-hand combat. The caption says that "Here English and French fell at the same time in battle". The Latin term used (*Franci*) reflects the composition of William's army, which, in addition to the ranks of Normans, contained soldiers from many regions across the Kingdom of France.

The Tapestry illustrates Harold's death – it shows the King falling to the ground after being struck on the thigh by a Norman knight. This detail is con-firmed by another written source, the poem by Guy of Amiens. The poet claims that William sent four knights with instructions to kill Harold. Guy of Amiens tells us that one of them hit him on the neck, another stabbed him in the chest, the third cut open his stomach and the last cut off his leg.

↑ Harold, wounded by an arrow, is struck down by a Norman knight (scene 57).

18

THE END OF THE TAPESTRY

The end of the Tapestry depicts the flight of the English, a scene which underwent extensive restoration in the 19th century. The Tapestry is clearly missing a final sequence which would bring the masterpiece to a satisfactory end. Various theories have been put forward to explain this abrupt ending. It is possible that the Tapestry was never finished because of the political changes in England from the 1070s onwards. Another theory is that the ends of the Tapestry were torn as a result of frequent rolling and unrolling over the centuries. If this is the case, we can attempt to piece together the missing scenes based on the poem by Baldric of Dol. This poem, which describes scenes that are identical to those in the Bayeux Tapestry, ends with the surrender of the towns of England and the coronation of William in Westminster Abbey on 25 December 1066.

This would give the Tapestry a coherent structure: at the beginning, the first scene represents King Edward in full royal pomp; in the middle we see the coronation of King Harold; and at the end it would therefore seem logical to show William crowned King of England, fully justified in this role by the "judgement of God" as expressed against Harold on the battlefield at Hastings.

↖ The first scene showing King Edward in full royal pomp may well have been matched by a similar final scene featuring King William. This direct succession was interrupted by Harold, who is shown in full royal pomp at the centre of the Tapestry.

THE WORK of art

The Bayeux Tapestry is a magnificent work of art that never fails to leave its mark on observers. But it is hard for us to appreciate its originality and nuances as we have no similar embroidered cloths that could serve as a point of comparison. The Tapestry is a remarkable example of narrative art composed of a series of scenes of varying lengths that recount a historical event. Each scene is set apart by its Latin *titulus* (caption), starting with the words *hic* ("here") or *ubi* ("where"), and by distinctive markings at the beginning and end (stylised trees, buildings and towers). The Latin captions serve as a commentary that enables us to identify the characters and understand the events. They are embroidered in dark blue wool yarn, except in the second part where red or yellow wool yarn is used for some letters.

↓ King Edward in full royal pomp (scene 1).

↑ Harold making his way to Bosham (scene 2).

The meeting between William and Guy of Ponthieu (scene 13).

SEPARATION AND CONTINUITY IN THE SCENES

The scenes in the Tapestry correspond to one of three main types. The first type is like an early version of the instant snapshot. Examples include scene 1, in which King Edward the Confessor sends Harold on the mission to Normandy, and scene 30, which shows Harold's coronation. In the second scene type, the characters move from one place to another in a continuous movement from left to right. This is the case for the scene in which Harold and his companions leave the royal palace to travel to Bosham (scene 2) and the Channel crossing from the port of Bosham to the banks of Le Ponthieu (scenes 4 to 6). The third type is more complex, depicting a meeting or clash between two characters or groups of characters. When William comes to free Harold after he is taken prisoner by Guy of Ponthieu, the two groups of people come face to face, one having arrived from Beaurain and the other from Rouen (scene 13).

The designers of the Bayeux Tapestry were also careful to link the scenes together if necessary to achieve continuity when depicting a rapid sequence of events. The comet with its *titulus* (*Isti mirant stellam* – These people marvel at the star), in the upper border, creates a close link between the fear felt by the English on seeing the comet and the anxiety of the King, who is warned of the threat of dramatic upheavals (scenes 34 and 35). Similarly, when Harold leaves for Bosham with his companions, the door of the royal palace remains open (we can clearly see the hinges) to link this scene with the previous scene when Harold is sent on his mission (scenes 1 and 2). This makes it clear that the figure opposite King Edward must be Harold. Sometimes, this continuity is shown by a complete lack of separation between two scenes. After the scene showing the oath at Bayeux (scene 23), two characters turn towards Harold, who is pledging his oath, but the position of their feet shows that they are preparing to board the ship. This implies that Harold returned to England immediately after making the oath.

↓ Harold returns to England (scene 24).

THE LOWER AND UPPER BORDERS

The historical account in the central part of the Bayeux Tapestry is framed by a lower and upper border, which contain a remarkable bestiary featuring real or imaginary animals. This colourful, diverse selection of animals has always been a source of fascination for visitors and historians alike and has raised numerous questions. How do these animals relate to the story that is told above or below? Do they have a particular symbolic meaning, as is often the case with medieval bestiaries? Do these animals serve as an ironic or critical commentary on the historical events, or are they simply a decorative technique, borrowed from the traditional panoply of limners and sculptors, with no particular allusion? However many theories are suggested as to their meaning, it seems that the borders of the Bayeux Tapestry are set to remain a source of mystery for many years to come.

We can make out domestic animals (dogs, horses, oxen and sheep), wild animals (lions, bears, camels, leopards and wolves) and imaginary animals (female centaurs, griffins and dragons). The animals are sometimes still and sometimes moving – the birds are shown flying, pecking, face to face or sleeping with their head under their wing. There is a clear reference to the fables of Phaedrus, inspired by those of Aesop: *The Wolf and the Lamb* (scene 4), *The Crow and the Fox* (scene 4), *The Lion with no Heir* (scene 5), *The Wolf and the Crane* (scenes 4/5), etc. It is worth noting that all these fables have morals that condemn treason and perfidy. And how should we interpret the five erotic scenes embroidered into these borders? They depict naked men and women, either alone or facing each other, but generally without any apparent link to the story in the central section.

TAPESTRY BESTIARY

Winged centaur

Falcon

Goat

Crow

Female centaur

Rooster

Camel

Dragon

24

Peacock

Lion

Fox

Winged lion

Swan

Leopard

Cat

Hyena

COMIC STRIP OR ANIMATED CARTOON?

The Bayeux Tapestry has sometimes been compared to a comic strip because of the way it is divided into separate scenes with captions. But even though this medieval embroidery tells a story in pictures, likening it to a comic strip hardly does it justice. The Bayeux Tapestry manages to depict several episodes and several moments of an event in a single scene, a technique that foreshadows animated cartoons or films. This saved time and space for the embroiderers and also served an aesthetic purpose. For example, the siege at Dinan took place in three stages (scene 19): the attack by the Norman knights (on the left), the threat of fire (in the centre) and the surrender of the town (on the right). There was no need to represent Dinan three times to indicate these three stages, because they could all be incorporated into a single scene.

The boat that arrives to inform William of Edward's death and Harold's coronation is designed in such a way that we can clearly see the three stages of the journey – boarding, crossing and berthing – within the same image (scene 34).

This technique for showing a chronological sequence within a single scene sometimes led the designers to depict the same person two or more times. When Harold sets sail for Normandy, the English Duke is represented no fewer than seven times. We see him seated at a table in his manor, then boarding the boat, with bare legs, holding his falcon; it is probably Harold that is at the helm of the ship; he is then shown at the bow, wondering whether to leave the vessel, and finally being captured by Guy of Ponthieu's men. The Bayeux Tapestry depicts the death of Harold's two brothers, Gyrth and Leofwine, who were killed at the Battle of Hastings.

↓ The three stages of the siege of Dinan (scene 19).

↑ Harold is represented twice, firstly being pierced in the eye by an arrow, then falling to the ground after being struck by a knight (scene 57).

Each is shown twice – once being struck, and a second time falling to the ground. The most striking example is Harold himself: we first see him with an arrow in his eye under the caption *HAROLD*, then falling backwards and dropping his sword as a Norman knight strikes a final blow to his thigh.

ENIT AD PEVENE SÆ :·

THE QUEST FOR PERSPECTIVE AND DEPTH OF FIELD

Although the Tapestry is a horizontal sequence of scenes that follow on from each other in a linear fashion, the designers were clearly at pains to create perspective and depth of field. The use of perspective is visible in the scene where the Normans begin pillaging the local area (scenes 41 and 42): at the top of the image, we can see two English houses that are smaller than the characters, suggesting a background in the distance. The same is true for the three small boats behind the larger boats in scene 38.

The artists also used two graphic techniques to create depth of field for the humans and animals. The first

was to embroider the horses' legs that were furthest away from the observer in a different colour from that used for the rest of the animal. In scene 52, for example, yellow horses are given two red, green or blue legs, creating a shadow effect that gives the impression of another dimension. The second technique was to use superposed images to depict boats, horses and people. William's boats during his Channel crossing are shown one in front of the other with a slight overlap so that only the bow or the stern is visible (scene 38). The horses are often presented in rows so that we can see just their hindquarters (scene 8)

↑ The ships are shown moving on four different planes (scene 38).

HIC EX

↓ Depth of field is created by superposed horses and men (scene 4).

or their heads (scene 18). At the start of the battle, the English are neatly arranged on eight successive planes (scene 51), giving the impression of a tightly knit, threatening group that is ready to do battle.

THE ART OF MOVEMENT AND LIFE

No people or animals in the Bayeux Tapestry are motionless or static. Everything in the illustrations points to movement and dynamism. The angle of the head, the position of the feet, a gesture with the hands and the use of frowns and other facial expressions all bring the figures to life, as we see in the very first scene with the sparkle in Edward's eye. But unfortunately, more often than not we find it hard to decode these subtle signs and grasp their full significance. The animals, just like the birds in the borders, are full of life. The designers show the horses walking, trotting, cantering and sometimes ambling. They move with their heads slightly bowed or fully lowered. Their manes billow in the wind, unless they have been cut short or twisted. Sometimes they are shown pawing the ground, anxious to get moving, like Turold's horses in scene 10. We even see them falling in spectacular fashion (scene 53). We see horror in the gestures of an English peasant when a Norman grabs him by the hair to kill him (scene 56). This constant animation turns the Tapestry into an epic poem, a pictorial version of a medieval *chanson de geste*.

↓ A spectacular fall involving three horses (scene 53).

↑This scene can be interpreted in two ways: for a Norman, Edward is urging Harold to keep his oath to William, whereas for an Englishman, Edward is conceding the royal throne to Harold (scene 27).

DELIBERATE AMBIGUITY?

Even after examining every last detail of the Bayeux Tapestry, countless mysteries and secrets inevitably escape our notice since we have lost most of the codes that help us decipher iconographic works of this kind. Moreover, some of the major scenes contain ambiguities which are not down to artistic shortcomings or interpretative difficulties. The ambiguity in certain key scenes of the narrative was a deliberate ploy that was cleverly used by the designers to convey the ultimate message of the Bayeux Tapestry. Many of the *tituli* are deliberately succinct, but if necessary they become much more detailed, for example in the episode at Mont Saint-Michel Bay, where, at great personal risk, "Duke Harold dragged them from the sand". In the scene showing Edward's death, we learn that "King Edward in bed speaks to his faithful followers", but the Tapestry tells us nothing of what he actually said, which would have been of vital importance. Similarly, in the scene where Harold pledges his oath, the caption simply tells us that he "made an oath to Duke William". Wouldn't there have been room to describe what the oath was about by adding a few words such as "about the royal crown" (*de corona regis*)? The aim of this cleverly maintained ambiguity seems to have been to enable two different interpretations of events, one by the English and one by the Normans – that way, both parties were kept happy!

In any event, the ultimate message of the Bayeux Tapestry was that William's victory on the battlefield at Hastings was granted by God, the Master of human history. And that conclusion is what gave the Conqueror his legitimacy, regardless of the merits of Harold, the English hero.

31

A WINDOW on life In the 11TH CenTURY

The aim of the commissioner and designers of the Bayeux Tapestry was to depict and shed light on the extraordinary events of 1066. In creating this work of art, they depicted people, animals and buildings by designing and embroidering what they saw around them, since they were portraying events that had only just happened. Historians and archaeologists therefore consider the Tapestry as a valuable first-hand account of life in the 11th century.

SHIPS

The Tapestry's creators depicted several ships, all of which are Scandinavian-type vessels that were well suited to sailing on the Channel, the North Sea and the Baltic Sea. They feature a raised bow and stern, often decorated with a dragon-like figure known in Old Norse as a *dreki* (plural *drakar*). The same term, spelt *Drakkar*, was coined again in the 19th century to refer to the ships themselves.

These ships were clinker-built; in other words, they were made using overlapping planks. They were propelled using sails or oars, which meant that they could make headway even if there was no wind. The Tapestry mostly shows warships (*langskip*) with twenty lines of rowers. These vessels were known as *snekkja*, from which the Old French term *esnèque*, used in Normandy, was derived. But the work also shows *knarr*-style cargo ships that

←A Scandinavian-type Norman vessel, with its distinctive continuous upper rim (scene 38).

:NAVIGIO:

were used to transport both goods and horses, of vital importance for the Norman army.

The ships depicted in the Tapestry are comparable with those that have been found in archaeological digs, especially in Scandinavia: the Oseberg ship (c. 820) and the Gokstad ship (c. 895), and the Roskilde and Skuldelev ships (11th century). These ships are in keeping with those in the Tapestry in every respect.

William's fleet was composed of more than a thousand ships. In scene 35, the Tapestry shows the entire ship-building process, from tree felling to floating the finished hull. We see ship-wrights hard at work with their axes. In reality, relatively few new ships were actually built: the Duke of Normandy requisitioned all the available boats in the ports around the duchy. A contemporary document, the *Ship List*, gives us an idea of the number of boats provided by William's most powerful vassals. William FitzOsbern and Hugh of Avranches each provided 60 ships, Odo of Bayeux 100 and Robert of Mortain 120, the highest number of anyone. The text adds that Duchess Matilda offered her husband a huge new ship, the *Mora*, with a figurehead representing a child playing a horn and pointing to England. This ship is represented on the Tapestry (scene 38) but the figurehead is shown at the stern.

→ **A cargo ship.**
Drawing by O. Crumlin-Pederson

↘ **A warship.**
Drawing by O. Crumlin-Pederson

↓ **The Oseberg ship.**
Oslo Viking Ship Museum

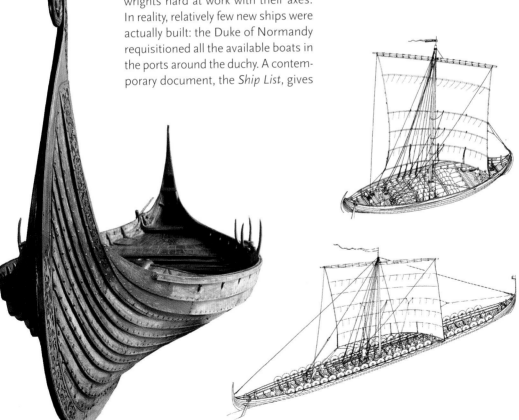

WEAPONS

The armies that crossed swords on the battlefield were composed of two categories of soldier. On the Norman side, the elite was formed of knights, and on the English side of *thegns*, as well as *housecarls* (of Scandinavian origin). The Normans and their allies fought on horseback, while the English did battle on foot. The Tapestry's designers particularly focused on these elite troops. The lower-level soldiers from the ordinary public are somewhat neglected in the illustrations. On the Norman side, we see archers but no infantrymen. On the English side, the peasants called up for the battle, which formed the *fyrd*, are shown.

The elite soldiers were equipped with the same weapons in both armies. The Tapestry shows this clearly, and it is undoubtedly an accurate reflection of the historical period.

The soldiers were protected by hauberks, helms and shields. The hauberk was either a coat of mail or, more likely, a leather garment to which iron plates were attached (as we can clearly see in scene 37). The conical helm included a nasal, but it didn't protect the entire face or even the eyes. The shield was generally oblong in shape. It was particularly designed for knights but was also used by the English foot soldiers, although some preferred to use a round shield.

The offensive weapons used by the Norman troops were lances and swords. The lance was the main weapon for the cavalry, who could

↙ The typical weapons of a Norman knight.

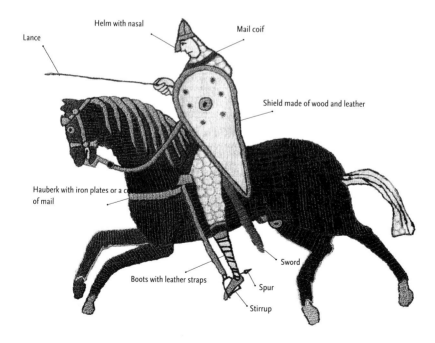

Helm with nasal

Lance

Mail coif

Shield made of wood and leather

Hauberk with iron plates or a coat of mail

Sword

Boots with leather straps

Spur

Stirrup

↑An oblong shield (Norman) and round shields (English) (scene 52).

↓Norman knights facing peasants from the *fyrd* (scene 53).

they also had very specific weapons: javelins, which were thrown at knights, and battle-axes, which were the distinctive weapons of the *housecarls*.

The lower-level soldiers were much less well armed. On the English side, the *fyrd* troops only used a lance and a shield. They were particularly vulnerable as they didn't wear hauberks or helms. The Norman archers were no better protected. On the Tapestry, they are only depicted at the beginning of the battle, in scene 51, and at the end, on the lower border.

The Tapestry gives precedence to the military elites, and especially the Norman and Frankish aristocrats, who fought on horseback. That explains why horses feature prominently, to such an extent that we might think the Tapestry's designer was a horse-lover.

wave it above their heads, hold it to their side or wedge it under their arms. The sword would have been drawn afterwards, for close-range combat. For a knight, a sword was a trusty companion with immense symbolic value. The English troops used swords, but

HORSES

The horses on the Tapestry are small – the riders' legs all dangle down well past their horse's belly. Some may have been Spanish horses, crossed with Barbs and Arabians. We can clearly see the horses' genitalia, which indicates that they were often stallions. In scene 48, for example, we see a groom presenting William with a magnificent charger with prominent genitals, symbolising force and controlled power.

The horses are shown with bridles and reins which the riders hold in their left hand, along with their shield strap. The wooden saddle, covered with leather, had a pommel and cantle. The knights wore boots with spurs, which were placed in long stirrups, giving them a good seat.

During the battle, the horses were subjected to a horrific ordeal: scene 53 shows four horses that have fallen over, providing the designer with a chance to show off his talent. The

↙A groom leads William to his superb charger (scene 48).

↑ Two knights at full gallop (scene 11).

↓ William leads the cavalry charge.

most spectacular is the "blue horse", which is lying with its head and neck to the ground and kicking the air with its hind legs. Many horses were killed in the battle, some of which are depicted in the lower border.

Although the main event depicted by the Tapestry is the battle, it also shows expeditions and castle sieges, giving us a glimpse of contemporary architecture.

The English are attacked by mounted Norman horses (scene 56).

ET CECI

MILITARY, CIVIL AND RELIGIOUS ARCHITECTURE

Scenes 16 to 19 portray the Norman army's expedition to Brittany, which led to sieges in the fortified towns of Dol, Rennes and Dinan. These strongholds are depicted as motte-and-bailey castles with wooden keeps surrounded by ditches. Archaeological digs have shown that fortifications of this type were common in the 11th century in Normandy and the surrounding area. The Normans had become masters in building these fortifications. In scene 45, we see them building a motte-and-bailey castle in Hastings from separate parts which they have transported by boat. After the battle, the Normans built fortifications of this sort in all the towns in England so that they could control them. They were subsequently converted to stone. The most famous of these castles is the Tower of London.

The Tapestry depicts the fortified towns of Rouen and Bayeux by their ramparts and castles (scenes 12 and 22). It also shows the interiors of urban palaces: the *aula* of the "Tour de Rouen" (Rouen Tower) in scene 14 and the interior of the Palace of Westminster in scenes 25 to 28. Although the embroidered images are highly stylised, we can see many characteristics that correspond to the conventions of Romanesque architecture, such as the arches in Harold's English manor and the blind arcades in the *aula* in Rouen.

The Tapestry features several religious buildings. While the little church of Bosham in England is represented symbolically, the newly built Westminster Abbey is illustrated realistically, with a small choir and a

→ St. Peter's Abbey, Westminster, dedicated on 28 December 1066 (scene 26).

← Bayeux Castle (scene 22).

hIC PORTA TVR : CORPVS · EADWARDI

→ Bosham church
(scene 3).

huge nave with tall arcades, separated by an imposing lantern tower. This building seems to have been based on Jumièges Abbey, which was being built at the same time. Robert, the former abbot of Jumièges, became Bishop of London and then Archbishop of Canterbury during King Edward's reign. This church was the setting for a solemn ceremony, the burial of a king. We see the body being carried by pall bearers, accompanied by choir-boys and singers – a real-life scene that brings us neatly to the Tapestry's depiction of daily life.

41

DAILY LIFE

The English and Norman characters in the Tapestry are shown wearing the same clothes, but we can tell them apart by their hair: the Normans have short hair and bare necks, while the English have long hair and moustaches. Clerics can be recognised by their tonsure but are otherwise dressed in the same way as the other figures (except when they are shown wearing liturgical vestments in scenes 28 and 30).

Most of the time, the men wear short long-sleeved tunics with a belt around the waist, which cover the body from the neck to the knees. The main social marker is the cloak, a garment worn by Norman and English aristocrats. The short cloak was worn for travelling, for example by William and Guy of Ponthieu when they met (scene 13). Long cloaks were reserved for ceremonious occasions and were generally held together by a brooch, either on the front or the side. Long robes were worn by kings or princes dressed in all their finery: Kings Edward and Harold, Duke William and Count Guy.

The main section of the Tapestry features only three women out of a cast of more than 600 characters! They are

←A noblewoman and her son are forced to flee when their manor is set on fire (scene 47).

ET hIC: MINISTRAVERVN hIC FECERVN: PRANDIVM: MINISTRI

↑The knights eat using their shields as tables (scenes 42-43).

↓The dignitaries' meal (scene 43).

Aelfgyva, Queen Edith and an anonymous English aristocrat who was a victim of the war (scenes 15, 27 and 47). These women are shown wearing long dresses and veils on their heads.

Table manners are portrayed on two occasions. At his manor in Bosham, Harold is the guest of honour at a dinner where horns are used as drinking vessels (scene 4). Further on, the Normans and their allies host an open-air meal, prepared by cooks and a baker (scenes 42-43). The way the different characters dine indicates their social status: the knights are given bread and chicken cooked on a spit which they eat standing up, using their shields as a table. The dignitaries, on the other hand, are shown sitting around a real semi-circular table eating fish and more sophisticated dishes. The food is served by a trained waiter. Bishop Odo blesses the bread, and this scene offers a compelling evocation of the Last Supper.

43

THE HISTORY OF the TAPESTRY from THE 11TH TO THE 21ST CENTURY

Little is known about the early history of the Tapestry. It was a portable work that could be taken down and stored in a chest (like the one that is still kept in the treasury of Bayeux Cathedral). It was probably displayed in various places, in great halls in castles and naves in churches, on both sides of the Channel. It is then thought to have come back to Bayeux Cathedral. It may have been on display in the Romanesque cathedral when the building was dedicated on 14 July 1077. But in reality we know nothing of the Tapestry's history until the 15th century. What is certain is that in 1476 it was kept in the cathedral treasury, as indicated by the inventory written at the time. The article relating to the Tapestry reads as follows:

↓ An engraving published by Bernard de Montfaucon, based on the copy by Antoine Benoît: Harold boarding his boat (scene 4).
BnF, ms fr 15635

44

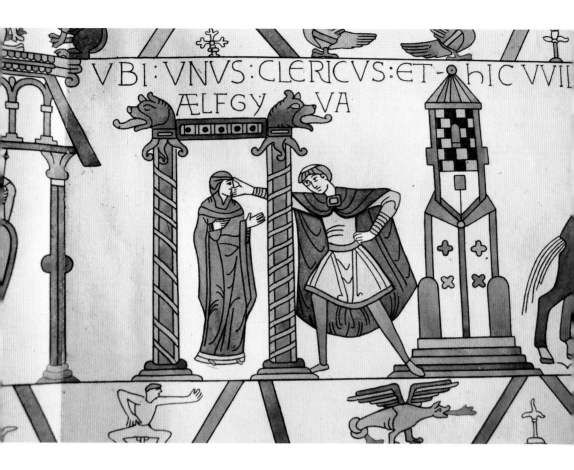

VBI : VNVS : CLERICVS : ET : hIC VVIL

ÆLFGYVA

"A very long and narrow hanging of linen, embroidered with figures and inscriptions representing the conquest of England, which is hung around the nave of the church [cathedral] on the Feast of Relics and throughout the Octave" (from 1 to 8 July).

In the 18th century, it was still displayed once a year. This was when it first came to the attention of the scholarly community. A first copy was commissioned by Nicolas-Joseph Foucault, Intendant of Caen (1689-1704). It caught the attention of a member of the Academy of Inscriptions and Literature, Antoine Lancelot, in 1724, then was noticed by a Benedictine scholar from the Congregation of Saint-Maur, Dom Bernard de Montfaucon. They each published a reproduction in 1729-1730.

The Tapestry came under threat during the French Revolution. In 1792, it had a narrow escape when an administrator for the District of Bayeux, Lambert Léonard Le Forestier, rescued it from revolutionaries who wanted to use it to cover their wagon. It was returned to the cathedral and was included among the goods of the clergy that were confiscated by the state. It was listed in the inventory

45

of the Arts Council in 1794. Under the Consulate, Napoleon Bonaparte, who was planning his own invasion of England, became interested in the work. He asked Dominique Vivant Denon, Director of the Napoleon Museum (now the Louvre), to have it brought to Paris, where it was displayed from November 1803 to February 1804. It was then returned and entrusted "to the inhabitants of the town of Bayeux".

From this point on, the work began to attract growing interest from scholars and travellers from France and England, including Gervais de la Rue and Amédée-Louis Léchaudé d'Anisy. Around the same time, Charles Stothard was sent to Bayeux to make a colour copy, which was published by the Society of Antiquaries of London.

In 1840, Prosper Mérimée had the Tapestry included on the first list of Historical Monuments. In 1842, the Tapestry was moved to a specially designed gallery in the Bayeux Town Library, on the Place du Château (now Place de Gaulle). The town's librarians became the Tapestry's curators. Several of them wrote articles or books about the Tapestry: Édouard Lambert (1842-1870), Jacques Laffetay (1870-1882), and later Simone Bertrand (1948-1978) and Sylvette Lemagnen (curator since 1989).

In 1913, the Tapestry was again relocated, this time to the former residence of the dean of the cathedral. It stayed there until the Second World War, when Hitler took an interest in the work. In 1941, he sent a group of experts led by Dr Herbert Jankuhn to study it. It was moved to the Château de Sourches, in Sarthe, for safekeeping, and was withdrawn in July 1944 to be sent to Germany. But it was still in Paris in August 1944 and was saved by the uprising. It was exhibited in the Louvre from 10 November to 15 December 1944, before being sent back to Bayeux for good.

In winter 1982-1983, a team of historians and textile specialists spent three months analysing the Tapestry. It was then relocated to its new home in the former seminary, which was renamed the William the Conqueror Centre. A new museum was built on the same premises after the town library moved elsewhere. For more than two centuries, the Bayeux Tapestry has been on display to the public, who flock in ever greater numbers from increasingly far-flung destinations to admire this remarkable work.

→ Queen Matilda embroidering the Bayeux Tapestry.
Musée d'Art et d'Histoire Baron-Gérard, Bayeux

Bibliography

Stenton (Sir Frank), ed., *The Bayeux Tapestry. A comprehensive survey*, London, Phaidon Press, 1957; French translation *La Tapisserie de Bayeux*, Paris, Flammarion, 1957; German translation, Cologne, Phaidon Verlag, 1957.

Wilson (David), *The Bayeux Tapestry*, London, Thames and Hudson, 1985; French translation *La Tapisserie de Bayeux*, Paris, Albin Michel, 1985.

Musset (Lucien), *La Tapisserie de Bayeux*, La Pierre-qui-Vire, Édition Zodiaque, 1989, republished Paris, 2002.

La Tapisserie de Bayeux: l'art de broder l'histoire, Proceedings of the conference in Cerisy-la-Salle, Pierre Bouet, Brian Levy and François Neveux (eds), Caen, Presses universitaires de Caen, 2004.

La Tapisserie de Bayeux: une chronique des temps vikings?, Proceedings of the Bayeux international conference (2007), Sylvette Lemagnen (ed.), Bonsecours, Éditions Point de vues, 2009.

The Bayeux Tapestry: New Approaches, Proceedings of a Conference at the British Museum, Michael J. Lewis, Gale R. Owen-Crocker and Dan Terkla (eds), Oxford/Oakville, Oxbow/David Brown, 2011.

Bouet (Pierre), *Hastings: 14 octobre 1066*, Paris, Tallandier, 2010.

Bouet (Pierre) and Neveux (François), *La Tapisserie de Bayeux, révélations et mystères d'une broderie du Moyen Âge*, Rennes, Editions Ouest-France, 2013.

We would like to thank the town of Bayeux, which gave us permission to reproduce images from the Bayeux Tapestry, and Sylvette Lemagnen, chief curator of the Tapestry, who gave us the benefit of her extensive knowledge of the work.

Editions OUEST-FRANCE
Lille – Rennes

Editor Matthieu Biberon • Editorial coordination Caroline Brou
Design Editions Ouest-France studio • Page layout and photo-engraving Graph&ti, Cesson-Sévigné (35)
Translation id2m • Cartography Patrick Mérienne • Printing SEPEC, Péronnas (01) - 08315171012
© 2015, Éditions Ouest-France, Édilarge SA, Rennes • ISBN 978-2-7373-6778-6 • Publisher number 7882.02.1,5.10.17
Legal deposit: May 2015 • Printed in France • www.editionsouestfrance.fr